CUTTING
APPLES

Cutting Apples

Jomé Rain

QUERENCIA

Querencia Press, LLC
Chicago, Illinois

QUERENCIA PRESS

LIBRARY OF CONGRESS CATALOGING-IN-PUBLICATION DATA

ISBN 978 1 959118 00 8

www.querenciapress.com

First Published in 2022

Querencia Press, LLC
Chicago IL

Printed & Bound in the United States of America

I am cutting apples. I think of you and my eyes grow wet. Why do my eyes grow wet? Did you do something to me? I am not angry at you; I am sad about you. My eyes sting. I am worried the apples won't come out well and I'll have to eat them anyway. I don't like to waste. Is that why I cling?

I am taking a course on the Ethics of Memory. I'm not sure what the point is yet. I will tell you when I figure it out, if you speak to me that day.

I have a lot of memories about you, but most of them are made up. Fantasized. My brain is tricky because she's good at making up stories, but after—I forget they are stories, I start to miss them like they were truths. So, did you love me? Or was that a story? And does it really matter, even a little bit? The you in my head loved me, and in a way, to me, that's the only 'you' that's ever existed.

Okay, then you loved me. I'm sorry. I didn't mean for you to do that. I love you, but I didn't want you to love me, too. It's dangerous to be a lover, because if you do it too well and the other person decides to make a go of it, then BOOM—you've lost your title. I am a natural lover, and the prerequisite of that is that I am always harboring affections unrequited. If you love me, don't requite me. Is that a word? Don't requite me.

I am trying to Drink Lots of Water. I stopped drinking alcohol, but I forgot to replace it with something, now my lips are always dry. Tell me to take a sip. Thanks. I didn't. Fuck. It's hard when there's no one around to hold me accountable, no one to perform for. At the beginning of this inside period, I didn't eat for two days. No one could tell me to do so, so I didn't. That's not a thing I have against food, I really like to eat. I just didn't see the point.

I am a person who likes to Cook for Others. I am what my (many) therapists have called A Provider. Usually this is followed up with a speech on Codependence and Trauma Responses. Usually, I stop listening by then. I am a Natural Provider. I don't feel comfortable with portion sizes. Whether I am cooking for myself or ten people, I always make too much. I am always expecting someone to walk in the door, a lone soldier stranded and needing a hot meal. I am a hot meal, too. But this is about the pasta.

Actually, I am not having pasta. I thought the word sounded better, but that's not what I am cooking. I am making rice. When the rice is done, it will be the turn of the apples, which will be sautéed until yummy and then cooked with shrimp. I am being experimental because I don't have anything else to do. Maybe when this is over, I'll write a cookbook. That would most likely be more interesting than this. People love words that tell them to do something. What am I telling you to do? Absolutely nothing. Be experimental, I guess. Masturbate in the shower. Why not? Big whoop.

I think I am in a mood. Not a bad one, just a one. My mom says that a lot, "I'm in a mood." Usually, when she says that, it's a bad one. Usually, when she says that, I've already noticed, and she is just Stating the Obvious.

I want to say something true now. I wasn't lying before, but now I want to say something especially true. My heart aches for no reason. False. There are many reasons. The trouble is finding them, excavating pain. I could do well with a shovel. This time I won't try to bash my head in. This time, I'm on a mission.

The trouble with giving up suicide is that when you're sad beyond comfort, there is nothing to look forward to. I used to fantasize about cutting my wrists open, now I'm jaded. That won't help, I know. So what? Stretch, meditate, write, repeat. Do you think this is helping my mental health or harming it? I don't know. That was an honest question. There! I found my truth.

The apples turned out well if you were wondering. I made a curry with apples, potatoes, and leeks. I added lots of spices, like cardamom, thyme, and curry. The shrimp didn't go, so I used leftover chicken. That was delicious.

It's nice to find use for things. As I said, I don't like to waste. Sometimes when I have leftovers in my fridge, it gives me anxiety. I worry about not eating the food, and the food getting sad, and growing mold. Is mold a symptom of sadness? If it were, I'd have been moldy by now, I think.

I'm not always sad. I'm not even sad right now. Does it sound like I am? Sometimes when I sound the happiest, I am actually quite sad. However I sound now, I am actually fairly content. I called Theo today to see if he'd like to come over. He called me a few days ago and said he would need to soon, because he's quarantined with his boyfriend who is Driving Him Crazy. No one has ever had to Drive Me Crazy, I've done well enough on my own. Is that a blessing? I guess no one ever has to drive another person crazy, but it still happens all the time. I'm happy to be alone, responsible for my sanity or lack of.

For now, I feel sane. I will need to take a break in a moment. I guess the break will be just for me, not for you. No matter how long I'm away, the next line will start, and nothing will be different to you, darling. Still, I'll let you know when there's a time break. Like the apples turning out, I think it's best that I keep you up to speed.

Good morning! There's been a time lapse. See? Told you I'd tell you. I ate my dinner and I did not return. Now I'm back. Hurrah! I've just woken up. It's not really morning, it's 13:27. That is afternoon. But my morning, yeah. I've been sleeping a lot, and deeply. It's funny, when I drink, I always wake up in the morning around 9am. I think that's because of the depressant/stimulant war that gets triggered by booze. It would seem when I'm sober, I have a lot more dreaming to do. I dreamt up a world very intricate yesterday, but I can't recall the details—only their shadows.

Last night you disappeared! I went to check on you and you were gone. So now I have your shadows, too. I wonder if this is a blessing in disguise. I spend a lot of time checking on you, making sure you still exist. Now I am not sure! Is this a gift? A gentle nudge? I remember once, you sent me a video of you in the bath, wearing all your clothes. You were upset because you did poorly on your exams. I remember thinking, "this boy is strange, and tender, and I will marry him one day." Some might argue that I have bad taste. Maybe you were trying to tell me that, too. If you were, I didn't hear you. Sorry about that. I've got too much love in my ears, it clogs up all the red flags ringing.

I am worried that I'm crazy. I read a quote "caring is not synonymous with crazy." That may be true, and though I took it as a comfort, I don't think the two are mutually exclusive. I may care, and I may be crazy. Hold on, I have to use the bathroom.

Back again. I am talking to a boy who I like. Notice I say like, and not love. Notice I say like, and not "am completely bonkers over." He's just a boy who is kind and I like, and like talking to. But I'm not gonna go crazy over him, which means I'll never fall in love with him. I only fall in love as a state juxtaposed with psychosis. Tepid feelings do not for good writing make. Unless?

Maybe I'll try something new. Maybe it's enough to be kind, and receive kindness, and laugh, and not be driven mad with that un—(possibly?)—requited nonsense. Maybe I'm too complicated for my own good. That's not really a maybe, I know that to be true. In order to be faithful, I have to be kept in a precarious state of constant unease and longing. The only lover I've ever been faithful to, wasn't my lover at all. You never touched me! But I stopped touching everyone else in hopes that you would. That's crazy. That's the Crazy I was referring, earlier.

I'm watching anime now. Michiko & Hatchin. That's what the Japanese version is called, in English it's "Finding Paradiso." But the English dub isn't great, so I'm watching it in Japanese. I usually watch anime in

Japanese, anyway. I don't mind the subtitles. Some people really hate subtitles, but I like them a lot.

Ellie is supposed to call me soon. I meant to call her yesterday, but I wasn't in the state. When she told me she would call, I found myself making up excuses—justifications for why I haven't worked on my collection.

"I'm not like you, E, I don't have all that energy."

"I've just been caught up in my head, I'm working on other things."

"It's hard to focus on one thing at once, for me."

Why does the idea of talking to a friend trigger the need to justify my own existence? All (most) of my friends are understanding. Am I not really just making excuses to myself, and pretending others are demanding them? So much of the pain that comes from other people's judgment of me is really my self-inflicted critique borrowing their voices in my head. Very rarely do people accuse me of the things I imagine them doing. So, it's all in my head, again. Big whoop.

My mother just texted the group chat. We are doing an Experiment in Abundance. We are trying to Change Our Perspectives. If I say 'big whoop' again, I'll be boring. *Big whoop.*

I'm not really as cynical as this text seems, but I put all my optimism into Doing and Talking. So, the cynicism, the boredom, the sadness—it doesn't get a healthy outlet. I guess this is a healthy outlet. I don't want to be a burden on people, so I tend to keep my mouth shut. Think Positive. Speak Rainbows. Lalalala. Boring. A bit. But it's for the best. If I've got all this shit in me, it's best for me to deal with it on my own time.

Overall, my mood has been good the past few days. I have been meditating a lot, which makes me happy. I feel so at peace when I meditate, sometimes I can't help but laugh or smile in the middle of it. And exercising! If I knew how good I'd feel from that, I wouldn't have skipped gym class as frequently as I did. Or maybe I would've. I guess I wasn't interested in Feeling Good back then. I was more interested in Feeling. Period. Mostly sad and lonely and pitiful. That's being a teenager, I guess.

Speaking of teenagers, I am consistently surprised that I am not one anymore. In a way, I still feel 16. Better adjusted, yes, but childish all the same. 22 is a strange age. It's a good number, but a weird age. I oscillate between wanting to be 16 and wanting to be 35. At 16, I was allowed to be carefree and have absolutely nothing figured out. By 35, I expect to be relatively stable and more comfortable with having absolutely nothing figured out, still. 22 is neither 16 nor 35, so I'm still in the eye of the storm.

Ellie just called me. Confirmation of my earlier suspicion, people have more to do than analyze and/or criticize me. Her and her boyfriend are having a fight. State Sanctioned Inside Time is hard on everyone, especially couples. The burgeoning apocalypse is not an ideal backdrop for Tender Loving.

They were arguing and he snatched the earphones out of her ears from behind. He was upset that she used his headphones to speak badly of him. When he took them out, the call ended. I felt a bit scared then, because the last image I had was of the snatching. She called me back and the call ended again. She's not picking up now. I don't think she's in danger, I think they're just fighting. But still, it isn't nice to see. I called her back and she didn't answer, and I've just texted her now. I am wondering if I should call the police. What do you do in a situation like this? If she doesn't respond in the next 10 minutes, I'll call the police. I don't know how to do that from France. I guess I'd have to have my mom do it.

Never mind, she's calling back. But he's still yelling in the background. She says she thought he had left, and she's going to call me back. I never know what pushes a man to graduate from yelling to hitting. It was always a very thin line, in my experience. So I'm scared for her, but she seems more angry than frightened.

It's later, again. Some hours. He did hit her, not when she called me then, but after. She kicked him out, she was crying when she called me. Not really crying, sobbing. I've never heard her like that. It was strange. She asked me to call him, and I did. I was planning to be angry, but when he picked up, I couldn't manage to. I asked him if he wanted to talk, and he said yes, that he really needed someone to talk to. I don't want to get into it all, but in the end, I think I did some good. I don't think he's a bad person, I think these are hard times. I don't want to sound like I'm making excuses for him—I'm not. There isn't ever an excuse to hit someone you love. But I didn't think being angry with him would help much, so I listened to him, and I spoke softly and in the end, I think he heard me. I called her back after and told her he'd leave her alone for a while and to take care of herself before she deals with her anger toward him. That's a quote actually, one of my favourites. I don't know who said it. "When you are hurt, before asking why, before seeking revenge, when you are hurt, before all: treat your wounds."

Right now, I don't feel wounded, so I'm not sure what to treat. I'm going to meditate again in a few minutes. I'm still watching that anime. I've just finished the second episode, now I'm on to the third. But I'll meditate first. I think meditation isn't just something to do when you're not feeling well, but also something to do when you feel good. With practice, it makes it easier to deal with the next time things get difficult.

I have no doubt that my meditation the past week or so helped me in the conversation with Ellie's boyfriend. Maybe if I was less calm, or drunk, or otherwise out of my head, I would've attacked him. I'm not sure, but it's possible. So, I meditate and stay sober and try to prepare for whatever comes next. Not just in this situation but in life.

Break time.

Sike! Austin (Ellie's boyfriend) called me right before I got up. So I've been on the phone with him for about an hour and a half, we just hung up. It was interesting to speak to him. Perspective is a funny thing, but sometimes all you need to do is speak. I wonder if Ellie will be angry with me for talking to him for so long. I'm never sure where to draw the line when someone I love is angry with another person. I wonder if love for one person really means denying it for another. I've been in situations before that told me that was the case—I've had friends create enemies and then expect me to go into the trenches with them. I don't know if I agree with that. Can anything really be resolved with hatred? Even when it seems so, the aftertaste always leaves me feeling nauseous. Truly, I only feel myself when I am compassionate. Any other avenue leads to guilt. So, what then? How to navigate in a world filled with anger? Even with my own, I feel the only way to work through it is to show compassion to my rage. To hold my fury with a tender hand, to allow it the space to scream and cry. Otherwise, I'd be burying it alive. And isn't that cruel, too?

I guess I'll pee now, it's been a while.

He called me again. I did have the time to pee, but just. I think I am doing good, but I worry I have caught myself in something that I can't extract myself from. It's not a bad thing, though. I have the time, and if I can help, I will. I just hope I'm helping.

I made some coffee, in anticipation of being up for a while. Why does coffee taste so much better in the hours after it's advisable to drink it? Most things feel better when they're inadvisable. Is that a word? I have 'Killing Me Softly' stuck in my head. Do you think that means something?

This isn't sounding the way it sounded earlier. I liked it better when I started. This is the problem with changing, you like yourself some days better than others. I wish I could like myself all the time. Maybe that's not human?

Before the quarantine started, I was never worried about people watching me through their windows. Now I am because people don't have anything better to do. I feel as if I'm in a display case, like a hamster in a pet store. A few days ago, I saw a very beautiful girl, naked in the window across the street. She was climbing into a mezzanine bed. I felt lucky that I had my contacts in, then I felt disgusting for looking, then I felt ashamed, thinking that someone might have seen me looking, and I made a very big deal of only looking around the room I was in from then on. But wouldn't the person who would've seen me look only been able to have judged me to the extent that they judged themselves for looking at me? Even so, if someone were watching me, they wouldn't know I was looking at the girl, unless it was her who caught me. Anyone from the other side of the street wouldn't know there was a beautiful naked woman getting into bed a few windows above them.

I'm practicing my Portuguese now. I'm not fluent in French yet, but I speak enough to get by, and I want to move to Portugal next. The plan has been to move to Porto at the beginning of the summer. I'm not sure if that plan will shift, given the state of the world. Speaking of climate, it's kinder in Portugal. Lots of rain, but warmer than Paris. I think it will be beautiful. I've actually been in Paris longer than I've been anywhere since I was 18.

I've liked it here the most, too—but I'm starting to get The Itch.

The Itch is an affliction bestowed upon all wandering fools/psycho-romantics. Moving can cure it for a short period, while everything is fresh and exciting in The New Place. But soon the New Place simply becomes The Place You Are In, and then it is only a matter of time before The Itch sets in. Usually I don't have a place in mind of where to go next, but it finds me fairly quickly. This is the first time I've gotten a destination stuck in my head like this, so I think it's wise to pay attention to it.

The good thing about The Itch is that once you've decided to move on, you can start enjoying The Place You Are In again, because we know it to truly be The Place You Are Leaving. So, Paris has since been injected with a newfound charm. I walk through the streets admiring the people and their culture, I look out the window and am warmed by the golden light hitting the buildings across. It's true (if It's been said), the light is special in Paris. This isn't the type of enchantment I had when I first wandered these streets and everything was new and enterprising, no. This is a different kind of admiration, the deep awareness of a city that will be left and doesn't know it yet. I smile as I walk, as if let in on a secret that no one but me is privy to. Paris, will you miss me? Will my absence be felt?

This is the same question I ask you, in my mind. Will you miss me? Do you miss me? Do you want me to miss you? Should you care if I went away? Why have you gone away? Are you alright? Hello?

The buildings of Paris have more answers for me than you do, of course. They're still listening (for now).

I wonder what you will think when you hear I've gone. I wonder if you'll even hear, if you'll care. I have been thinking about deleting my Instagram—that doesn't have to do with you though. I am simply thinking that I'd like to exist a little bit less. That isn't a suicidal nor depressive ideation. I have just been thinking of taking up less digital space and committing to more real-life presence. Can I see a friend without documenting it? Can I have a thought without sharing it? Do I need to make myself jealous or participate in the endless discourse that is the ever-growing matrix? Should I see what it's in front of me, and say things out loud or to a page? I want to delete my online presence because it frightens me to think of it, and I want to do more things that frighten me. Quitting drinking frightened me, once upon a time. Then it got to be scarier to think of what would happen if I didn't. It's starting to look the same for other things, though I won't say all of them out loud. I still need time to think.

So, Instagram is on its way to being deleted, but I need to wait for better Wi-Fi to do it. That may seem counterintuitive, but I need to wait to download all my data. Did you know you could request that? It takes a day or two, but if you ask, Instagram will send you a file of all the data associated with your account—photos and messages, etc. I want to keep a record of that, because I think I might want to use it for art sometime later. I once deleted all the photos off my Instagram because I was enchanted by a boy who told me it was the right thing to do, and I mourn those records often. Nearly 5 years of memories, flushed. I miss them, dearly. Maybe they'll be in the data pack, fingers crossed. I think nostalgia is underrated. It's nice to look back, sometimes. More often than not, the things I've felt needed to be erased have become fond memories once I've had some distance. I try to remind myself of that now, when I think of where I am.

I was thinking yesterday about Eternal Sunshine of the Spotless Mind. It was related to that course in The Ethics of Memory. I wondered if I would delete a person from my mind if I could. I thought about you. I daydreamt about meeting you some years from now, in some new city, completely oblivious to what you've meant to me. I thought about you greeting me, and my knowing nothing of you—you moving on, confused. And then I thought about you approaching me some days later, asking if I remembered you. And I'd say, "Of course I remember you, you're that beautiful boy from the shop a few days ago." And you wouldn't know what to do, and I'd be confused, and maybe I'd fall in love with you all over again anyway. I shook myself out of that fantasy because I didn't think it was a Loving Thought. In a very underhand sort of way, it was a revenge fantasy. I don't want revenge (for what, even?) and I don't want to forget you. I guess though, I'd like to run into you at a shop.

Good evening! It is tomorrow. A full day has passed but I haven't slept, so my eyes are feeling heavy now. I spent the whole day waiting for the sun to go down. Now, in the hours before it sets, I feel moved to action. I got up and cleaned the apartment, did some light exercise and a meditation—now I'm writing here. I am going to need to call my mother shortly. That's the prompt for today's meditation. I need to ask her some fairly personal questions, nothing extraordinary but still intimate—I'm nervous that I won't be able to connect with her on account of my sleep deprivation. But I don't want to put it off until tomorrow, so here is my warmup to practice stringing words together. I haven't done it yet.

I spent the entire morning and afternoon (it's 7:30 pm now) rewatching Sherlock. Each episode is an hour and a half, so I've watched about 15 hours straight. That's not something I do often, but it's what I did today. Sometimes it feels nice to escape into adventures when I can't have my own. About halfway through my binge, I started to Self-Analyze its cause, and my deduction was: I am craving adventure. Maybe my wild woman is calling out to me through the channel of a detective series, begging me to find my own mysteries to unravel. I guess I have been a bit bored.

Sometimes I dream up adventures while I'm awake, my eyes are open, but I am Elsewhere. I love that word, it's so pretty. I think the sleep deprivation is definitely getting to me now. I'm going to call my mother anyway. One of my (relatively new) rules is that when I make a choice that I might regret (i.e., staying up all night), I still have to do the things I was meant to do otherwise—usually the consequence of not doing them is why I feel badly about the first choice. So, if I decide to get lost in a drama for an entire day, that's fine, but I've still got to do the things I was planning to do before I made that decision. Maybe that's maturity. It used to be that when I stayed up all night and had school or work the next morning, I'd wake up (if I'd wake up) feeling completely powerless to do any of it and end up going back to sleep. For the past year or so, I've been really good about rising to the morning challenge (even if the morning is really afternoon). That's a layer of progress I'm happy to see. I don't know if I'll ever fully cut out staying up all of some nights, I believe that's intrinsic to my nature—and a lot of creativity has come from that trait—but I do think it's happened less often since I realized it wasn't an excuse I could use in adult life for being a shithead the next day.

I wonder if I'll look back at this time and feel pity for being so hard on myself mentally. I'm not always hard on myself, but I am usually. Lots of people tell me that. I just don't know if there's room to get better while also being gentle with myself. Sometimes, yes—of course. But sometimes, being hard on myself is a good kick in the ass toward tangible action. I guess it's a balance. I oscillate throughout the day, by any rate. Maybe I'm just overthinking. I have an intense fear of denial, it's a trait that I observe by the bucket-load in both of my parents, and I see it in myself sometimes too.

So, I try to dive in when I notice denial, to strip it away and get to work so it doesn't eat me up by the time I'm older. Of course, I'm always getting older, but I mean much older. Their ages, I guess. Age is strange. At some point I was a baby, and I was a blink of a percentage of my mother's age. And now it's now, and I'm nearly half it. And later, I'll be more than half of it—meaning we'll have spent more time alive together than she will have lived without me. Actually, that's next year for my mom. I still have a few more to half my dad or Jeremiah. Again, and more bluntly: age and time are absolute mindfucks.

I just got off the phone with my mom. We spoke for an hour, the time passed quickly. For today's meditation prompt, I had to ask her these two questions which were a bit loaded, and I felt emotional when she answered them. I felt sad, but not in my eyes, deep in my belly. Then it came up to my eyes, though I didn't cry. I often come close to crying without actually having tears spill. I have to be feeling really, truly fucked up to cry. I didn't feel really, truly fucked up just now, I just felt a sort of lazy sadness—the kind that ebbs and flows without threatening to open the floodgates. I took notes, so I'll write them here.

Question One: What has been your biggest pain or disappointment of your life so far?

"Myself. Not living up to my potential, making some really bad choices that could've been prevented. Not holding high expectations of myself, even though others did. Getting lost in the world and not making enough effort to get to know myself and discover my passions."

I felt very sad when she said that, but I buried the feeling under this clinical mindset I often take on when I have emotional talks with my mom. I don't do it nearly as much with other people, but people who I'm extremely close/volatile with—i.e., my mother or my lovers—I have a tendency to give the controller over to my brain, even when my heart is screaming or singing very loudly. That's a defense mechanism, right? Big whoop. Do I even need a therapist?

Question Two: What is your greatest dream/desire that remains unfulfilled?

"That has changed a lot over the last few years. Mainly, I wish that people would forgive me. Separate people and incidents, I've tried to make amends...And I want you to find love, for a long amount of time...I want you to fall in love with someone for more than their body. I want you to find love the way I love you."

Me: "I think I might have to have a kid to do that."

"Yeah, maybe you're right. Not yet though!"

More emotions. Lalala. Yes, definitely a defense mechanism. It will probably hit me later, when I'm not trying to document. Right now, I want to be clear and true. My feelings are rarely the first, and it's debatable about the latter.

Wait, I'm not sure what that means. Aren't all feelings true? Even if they're just covering up other feelings, that doesn't make the surface feelings less authentic.

I noticed that between both of my mother's answers, an overarching theme was guilt. It's funny, a few days ago we had the task of identifying five traits within ourselves that limit us. Two of my five were guilt and escapism. The other three are a secret. You don't know me well enough for that kind of info. Or maybe you do, in which case you probably don't need any hints.

So, guilt and escapism. Those are two things I heard mirrored in my mother's words—losing yourself in the flow of life and other people, not taking the time to know yourself because those two things are very interesting distractions on the road to self-referral....and that echoed a fear I have constantly: taking up too much of my time focusing on love and friendship and not taking the time to get to know myself and to learn to like that self. I've done it in the past for long stretches of time. Most of my teenage years, honestly. Maybe I saw that guilt in my mom before she said it so plainly, and I have been reeling in response, trying to find a way to avoid that same trap. I want to have my own guilt when I'm older, I don't want to renew the cycle. So, now I'm trying to spend time with myself, figure out what I like, experiment, learn, fall in love (platonic or romantic—same thing for me, mostly) without losing myself.

Sometimes I feel overly cold when I look to my parents' lives for tips on where I need to start digging within myself, it feels like a sort of exploitation. I know it's not, really. If I didn't try to learn from my parents' mistakes, I'd be wasting them. But I wish there was a way to dive into this work without feeling like I'm leaving my mother behind. I know that's irrational and a bit narcissistic, but it's a childish way of looking at things and I am, indeed, childish. I still have it in my head that my actions are directly responsible for my parents' wellbeing, like a kid who thinks their parents are divorcing because of something they, themself did.

But it's never really like that. We're all responsible for our own shit, and we can't place that on another person. It's not fair for me to be angry with my parents for giving me shit to deal with. It's mine now, and I'll have to do it or be majorly bummed later in life if I (surprise!) still have to do it.

By the way, as often as I am angry with my parents for Giving Me Shit, I am twice as often grateful and happy to have incarnated as their daughter.

I've got a lot more Sweet than Shit bubbling around in here. That combination of the two, is that what people mean by 'umami'?

It is tomorrow again. It is always either today or tomorrow. I guess it's both at once, now. So, it's tomorrow, and it's today.

I woke up at 3:30 pm, it's 4 now. I woke up with a cloud between my eyebrows, the fuzzy kind. I woke up wondering why I felt so fuzzy. I think it was because I took a sleeping pill last night. I was trying to reset my schedule, but I woke up too late, so I tricked myself a bit. I really needed the sleep.

I dreamt of a beautiful boy—I know I've seen him before, but I can't recall from where. We were on a bus. I was on the bus, going somewhere high up. He got on the bus, and we made eye contact. I thought he would sit next to me, but he sat at the front. But later he came and sat with me, he took the inner seat, next to the window. I had been looking for bonding glue with Suki earlier, to fix our shoes. I had a new pair of Doc Martens, but the sole was coming off already. When he sat next to me, he fussed around in his bag and took out the glue I was looking for, he put a little on his fingertip and then transferred it to my own. We were both smiling, and I fixed my shoe, rubbing my fingers in the middle part that attached my sole to the shoe. But then the whole sole came off, and I was embarrassed to ask for more glue. I don't remember what happened after that. He was very beautiful, though.

He was tall and brown skinned, with very kind eyes. He reminded me a bit of Alex from Beauvais, if he were black. I think the boy was mixed, black and some kind of East Asian. I remember thinking in the dream, "I know you!" But I don't know now if I was thinking of him to be Alex, or if I've seen him somewhere before.

Sometimes I feel like my dreams are doing a major psychological clean up, and I wonder if I would be better off sleeping for a week straight to give my subconscious the time to arrange itself. I fantasize about that sometimes, living in a dream world. I would like to learn to lucid dream, but I'm worried that I'd get addicted to it somehow. Anything that I can get addicted to, I usually do. I have an Addictive Personality. I think it's a two-way street. I get addicted to lots of things, and lots of things get addicted to me. The latter confuses me sometimes, when I see it in action. I don't think I'm a fun addiction, more a masochistic one. It's silly to get addicted to a person. They'll most likely disappoint you and ruin your high. That doesn't mean it's bad to love, but it's bad to get addicted to love. I'm a bit of a love addict, too. You would tell me that. The You in my head always tells me that. I don't argue, because I like to hear your voice. Sometimes the You in my head insults me, tells me I'm a mess, sometimes I talk back then—imagine myself saying My Side of the Story. "I'm not crazy, I just care too much." You always laugh, and I like the sound.

I think I need to leave the house today. I haven't left the house in six days, last week to do my grocery shopping. This morning I checked my bank account and saw I'd gotten paid again, so I guess it's time to do the shopping. I think I've spent less money in the past two weeks than I have for any two-week period in the last three years. I don't know why I said three years, it could be more or less—the point is: I usually spend a lot of money.

I am not a person who saves money. I am a person who believes there is always more on the way. To be fair, there is always more on the way, one way or another. I often go from having absolutely no money to my name, to having more than most people my age, in a matter of hours. I guess escorting makes you spoiled, has made me spoiled. Even before though, I was never good with money. I've always been a little loose, in all aspects of myself.

You are still gone, by the way. That's a few days now, no withdrawal symptoms yet. To be fair, you were Gone From Me before you were Gone—so there's not much to adjust to; only now I can't look at your altar to remember you. That sounded strange. I was trying to be poetic, but I don't want it to sound like I have an altar to you. For clarity: by altar, I was referring to your Instagram. Somewhat luckily (or not, depending on your stance on the subject), I do have some photos of you on my phone, so if the missing gets bad, I am free to refer to them. I have yet to refer to them. There's not really much need to—I can recall them by memory.

I have a thing in my brain that works differently. It's hard (nearly impossible) for me to picture things. I can think of a red apple, but I don't see a red apple—I have to describe to myself what a red apple looks like and focus very, very hard to get the shape in my mind. Still when I get it, it is incredibly foggy and distant. I can't bring it into focus, and it doesn't really look like an apple. When I picture my mother, I receive the emotions related to my mother—I get launched into memories including her, but I don't see her face. I hold the idea of her face, I know what she looks like, but if you were to ask me to describe it, I'd fall flat. Still, some things are easier to recall than others. I can remember more details about the photo of you sitting by the typewriter than I can about my mother's face. Go figure.

I don't know why I write to you as if you'll ever read this. I would never, ever let you read this. Things I've learned from a (short) life as a writer: if you want someone to love you, there are some parts of you they cannot read. I know that doesn't sound healthy, but whatever. I am a very romantic person, and I do believe that we should be able to be completely honest about ourselves—that we are still deserving of love as we are. I, romantically believe that, but in practice, it is not always the case. In fact, most often it is not.

I am honest about every part of myself, but I divide that honesty up among different people. It's like having horcruxes. I give a piece of my heart and my truth to different loved ones, but if I gave it all to one, they could kill me. I have, and they did. I have died before from trusting too much, being too idealistic about truth telling. I'm not afraid of The Big Death, because I've died many little times, and each time I got up, a little worse for wear but still a little wiser. By little deaths, I am not referring to orgasms—though I've had a lot of those too. Little deaths are moments in which a piece of you burns all the way up. Sometimes it is a big piece, and I feel I'll never be able to go on without it, so I die. Sometimes I have a funeral, I write a eulogy, I pray over the death inside me, before me. And then I get up, and some new part grows like a hydra, and I march out to be killed again.

Here's a list of some places that I've died:

&< Downtown Los Angeles, California
&< Tarzana, California
&< Harlem, NYC
&< East Village, NYC
&< Bushwick, NYC
&< Kensington, London

✂ Bermondsey, London
✂ St James' Park, London
✂ Île Saint-Louis, Paris

That list is not exhaustive, and some places listed contain more than one death. Downtown Los Angeles, for example—there were two there. I've gotten more ceremonious with my deaths, and they're starting to have more space in between them. I'm also not afraid of them anymore. Each time I die, I become a little better, like a morbid wine. Does this sound morbid? I'm not trying to be. I guess I'm a little dramatic and death obsessed, but at least I'm not frightened. Some obsessions, some compulsions are truly frightening. Death is not one of them, and neither are you.

I am crying now. It's later, 9 pm. I am crying because I was just talking to my mom, and now I feel overwhelmed and frustrated. I am trying to Stay Present, but in the present, I am crying. Wonderful. The week before last I Googled "how to cry more". Now I am crying, and I'm confused as to why I would've wanted to. I guess I was hoping for more of an intentional cry of release rather than a childish cry of frustration and anger only masquerading as sadness. I'm going to meditate, but I just wanted to check in to say that this is The Present and I Am Crying.

Never mind. Let's dive in, let meditation wait. If I meditated right now, I think I'd be using it as a means of escape, which is the opposite of the practice I've been trying to create. So, I am crying, let's lean in. I am crying because I feel guilty. I feel like a bad daughter. I feel guilty for not calling my father and for not noticing that I hadn't been calling my father and for calling my mother three times a day and for continuing to call her even when calling her leaves me feeling upset or unwanted. I am crying because I am frustrated with the codependent cycle that is my relationship to her. I am crying because I love her and that feels like hatred sometimes because the mother that I love also died a long time ago and the one who's replaced her can be quite the cunt. Note: Dying many times in one life runs in my family. My mother died many times before she had me, and probably again when she had me, and many times thereafter. My mother is often Unrecognizable to me but I'm still waiting for the last good version to come back. That is mean, and it's also true (though not always). I am guilty and sad for not being a daughter who calls when she's meant to and cares the appropriate amount and doesn't get sucked into feeling as though I'm being manipulated by the people who raised me. I am angry because quite often, I am being manipulated by the people who raised me, even if they don't notice. I am sad because life is made of manipulations, and I am sad because I'm no fucking good at them. I am sad because I am crying, and that only makes me cry more. I am sad because I feel embarrassed of being made to cry by a woman who had no intention to have that effect on me and has also possibly and probably lost her mind. I am sad that my mother is crazy and my father is crazy and I'm a product of them both, so I must be fucking bonkers by design. I am sad because I keep making strides to un-crazy myself and I can only get so far before the tree comes knocking to remind me that I'm an apple.

I have a memory from when I was younger. I'm not sure how old, but I must've been under 10 because it takes place in my bedroom in my father's apartment in Los Angeles. I remember that my father could go from talking to screaming at a moment's notice if I pushed too far or was too much. Screaming is not the right word, that implies a sort of hysteria. Yelling? Not quite. There is a noise that comes out of my father when he is angry, it is louder than a voice, it feels like a BOOM. Okay, he was booming? I'm not sure that's right, but it's the closest I can come. I can describe his voice when he goes BOOM! but it won't explain the feeling of hearing it. It is a sound that makes you feel very, very, very small, even now when I remember it—I feel teeny tiny. It is a BOOM! that makes you feel very tiny and like you should not move because maybe the creature making the BOOM! will not see you then.

Okay, so the memory. I think my father was booming, I was getting BOOM!'d at for some reason or another and I went into my room. I remember sitting on the floor with my back to the wall and my knees drawn up to my chest. I was hitting myself, closed fists against my skull. I just kept hitting myself. I don't know for how long. That's all I remember. I know I did that many times, but that's the memory I kept. I feel now how I felt then. My dad hit me sometimes, but he also didn't have to. If I felt how I feel now, powerless and frustrated, scared and angry— whenever I felt is way, I would just hit myself. And later, as a teenager, I started to cut myself. And my parents asked why—they couldn't see where it was coming from. But I had been doing it all my life! All my life spent hurting myself because of frustration I could not process and transgressions I did not understand but was most certainly guilty of. And now I don't hurt myself, but I still feel guilty. I still feel like I deserve it.

As I said earlier on, I'm not always sad. I'm not even usually sad. There is, however, an underlying sadness that weaves through everything I do, everything I say. A lot of people have that. If you listen closely, you can hear it when they speak. I can hear it, at least. It sounds like my parents. I think they're sad, too.

On days like this, I become frightened to have children. More specifically, I become frightened to be a mother. To hit the nail on the head: I am absolutely terrified of becoming my parents.

My mom was the age I am now when she got pregnant with me. Sometimes I feel guilty that she kept me. Sometimes I picture my parents' lives if I hadn't been born, and it's hard to convince myself that they wouldn't have been better off. This is not a commentary on my worth as a person, this is a commentary on how fucked things can get from a little change of plans.

I have decided: You are not a person, You are a feeling.

I was just reading through our old messages. I don't know why I do that. Or rather, I didn't know why I do that. Now, I think I do. It's a feeling! Isn't that what nostalgia is? Not longing for the past specifically, but longing for the feeling we associate with a time remembered? Honestly, the memories that I'm reliving were awful the first time around, but remembered, they make me feel giggly. I think maybe it's because I was younger, not much, but still. Youth is a drug in a way, and I get a bit high when I trigger its memories. I'm still young, I know, but I'm older. I wrote a piece once that describes this feeling, the nostalgia for shitty times. Hold on, I'm going to find it.

I fell asleep. Now, I am thinking. I am wondering: is it possible?

I am thinking of mourning, shapeshifting, burial, etc. I am thinking of the parts of myself I would like to hold a funeral for next. I am thinking of quitting certain things and picking up other ones. Okay, drinking: done. Work in progress, more like. Smoking? Could that be next?

Let me clarify. I am thinking of dying, but not all the way. I am thinking of killing the parts of myself that are the basis of my existence. I am thinking, okay—what if I were healthy? What if I worked out, and didn't smoke, and listened to happy music instead of sad love songs that bring me back to you?

Theory: If I kill the girl I was when I fell in love with you, maybe the love would die with her. Maybe, if I change, the next time I see you, it won't affect me at all. I could look at you like a memory of a past life.

Can you kill longing? Right now I miss you all the time—I think because I am close to the girl who decided you were The One. But if I change, won't the definition of who that is change too? If I were different, if I were Safe and Sane, maybe The One would be too.

I don't even know where to start. The girl I am now is afraid of not loving you because she thinks that is where the art comes from.

I am crying because I had a dream you were breaking, and now I am worried you're dead. I know you're not dead, but that does not ease the worry. I am crying because I am frustrated, again. I am a ball of stress. A big ball of yarn that is threaded with anxiety.

I got Ellie to check on you. A screenshot of your response tells me "I'm doing ok💖💗". This is not okay. You may be okay, but I don't feel okay for asking through the grapevine. I had a dream that you were breaking, and I've been shaking all day. Okay, you're 'ok.' Okay, I think I am not. So what? What should I do? What am I ever supposed to do?

I'm going to take a shower.

Before I do, a thought. I used to say that I felt like Jean Grey. She had these walls put up in her head by Professor X to keep her from turning into Dark Phoenix. I still feel like that a lot of the time. Sometimes I can feel something behind a wall, I push and push for truth and instead I am left with a migraine. There are answers within my skull that are hiding from me and I don't know how to coax them out. I've tried to flood them with booze and tears, I've tried to bore them with stillness and health.

Again, I don't know what to do.

I feel better. I'm not sure why, but I do. I like to peel my nail polish off in one strip. That is a simple pleasure. There are others, too.

Ingvild sent me an email last night, in response to the one I sent her a few days ago. It was very beautiful. I sent her the first chunk of this document on the first day I started it, and she sent me a stream of consciousness letter in return. She sounds like a fairy over text. She appears as a fairy in person, but it's different through her writing. Her voice is like strawberries, that's the only way to describe it. In person she has the fire within her, but over text it's more like a warm bath. A distillation of self? I love the way she writes, and I love her as well. She's the first person I've loved both poetically and in practice.

She sent me a pdf of George Orwell's "Why I Write" because it reminded her of something she said in her email. I like what she said, but I didn't like his piece all that much. It's very hard for me to like literary discourse, though I love literature. The only thing I've found so far that I liked on the subject was Margaret Atwood's "Negotiating with the Dead."

Loving you is a ritual. One I am quite attached to.

Ellie has made the suggestion of thinking of you as a symbol. I've done it before, but I've never thought of it so simply. Yes, you are a symbol to me. You are karmic in many ways, a love story that I have birthed, nurtured, and now refuse to let go of, even if you do not participate. You are a salve made of my father's rejection and an antidote to my mother's codependence. I use your image as a tonic, a cleanse—I drink you up and flush my toxins. Again, again. What do I want from you? Nothing but knowledge. I want to want nothing from you. Somehow, you are teaching me to want nothing. Loving a person should be enough. In fact, it is. Sometimes I forget that. Sometimes I get caught up in the wanting of return, but where's the purity in that? I want to love purely, I've said that is my mission, I've heard it whispered through dreams and intuition. So, who better to teach me? I've met you before, I'm sure. A lesson to be learned, again. Maybe I didn't fully get it last time around. This time, be still. I have to be still. I have to let you be who you are and love you for it and never expect you to do the same. This does not mean that I give you my all and expect nothing in return. I cannot give you my all, and I should not. I can only give you what I am moved to offer, and it has to be pure—it has to come without expectation, or it will not be a gift, but a trap. I don't want to lay traps, I don't want to try to force love from another. I want to give it for no reason other than that it is within me and it is begging to be shared.

I have to type quickly so my brain cannot outrun my fingertips. When I think too much, I lose the truth of what must be said so sometimes I type with my eyes closed. I can go back to fix grammar, add punctuation later, but in the moment, I must bleed onto the page. It does not hurt to bleed this way. For once bloodshed is self-care instead of harm.

I do not want to harm myself anymore. I am trying my best to leave the blade in the kitchen and use my fingers to move the pain within me. It's working, somehow. Sometimes I forget that it is working, or I do not notice the progress I am making, but when I look back, I know that I have worked hard to become the woman I am now.

It's strange that I just called myself a woman. I never think of myself that way. In so many ways, I am still a girl. But I am no longer the girl-child I was. Now I am half girl, half woman. Will that change? Will I ever lose my girlhood? I don't want to. I love being a girl, the idea of being a woman frightens me. I know many great women. Ellie is one of them, the closest to me. I am ashamed that I did not say that of my mother. I know that if I want to be love, I will have to be gentle with her. I will have to heal the parts of myself that are angry with my mother or

I will never be able to fully embrace myself. She is me, after all. At least in part, and I am her in many ways. So, I hold anger for my mother and that anger turns into distaste for myself. I see aspects of her within me and I shrink back, I hiss in their direction. I cannot be angry forever. Or rather, I very well could, but I don't want to be.

How do you forgive someone? I've done it many times without thinking, many people who I've been told did not deserve my forgiveness have received it without a second thought. But how do you forgive someone who you do not understand? I do not understand my mother. I understand her more than most people do, and yet I do not understand her, because I do not understand myself. Or rather, I do not accept her. I think I do understand her, but I refuse to accept what I understand. If I accepted her, then it would mean that before she is my mother, she is a person deserving of unconditional love. And I would have to know that it is my duty to set the boundaries I never created as a child, and that would be a loving act. But I am addicted to her. Is that strange? I am angry with her, and I hate to think I'm like her, but I'm addicted to her. I rarely make a decision without consulting her first. If there's a problem in my life, I call her. She is always there, even if she is not always kind. And she knows more about me than any person on this earth, than most people on this earth combined. I suppose my mother is my most dangerous horcrux, but there are still things that even she doesn't know.

It's funny how when I write about you, the subject so quickly turns to my mother. I thought you represented my father, but that's not where you lead me. What are you trying to show me here? I wish you'd speak up. It's no fun to solve a mystery by myself. I am both the client, the case, and the detective. I thought you could at least be Watson. Maybe you are, in an absentee way. Sorry for the Sherlock reference, it's still stuck in my head.

Thalie suggested I astral project to you tonight. I told her I've been trying. Which is true, actually. I have been trying to astral project these past few days. I haven't been trying with the purpose of seeing you, though. I think that would be a bit strange. I have more of an inclination to meet someone who can tell me what the fuck is going on.

I wish I meant what's going on in the world. I wish I were so selfless. I want to meet my personal guides, who can tell me where to dig on this path to self-knowledge. I have so many theories, but I know very little about myself for sure. I would like some assurance.

Does that make me selfish? I genuinely believe I will do good for this world when I've mucked out my own stall. I am worried that if I carry these things within me all my life without understanding them, I won't be able to do what I came here for. I would like some help.

Sometimes I talk to the stars. I've cried looking at them, and I always say the same thing: "I want to go home. I miss you. I want to come home." And my back gets warm. That's a symbol for when I've said or thought something true. Sometimes I just let the warmth in my back guide me. If I have a decision to make, I say all possible solutions in my head and wait for one to warm my back. It always works, but I'm not sure if it's psychosomatic. Sometimes I'll hear a voice in my head, it's much more peaceful than my thinking voice, and she always says things that are very simple and pure. When she speaks, I get the warmth in my back, and I know it's not my brain trying to trick me. It's my voice and it isn't. It's not my voice, it's My Voice. It's like a version of me without turmoil. I like her. I'm looking for her, I'm on my way to her always. I hope this is taking me there.

I have really got to stop waking up at 3 pm. I think tonight I will take a sleeping pill at 8pm. That way, even if I sleep 14 hours, I will wake up at 10am the latest. I like waking up in the mornings. I always feel a bit shitty when I wake up in the afternoon, as if I've missed something. Considering the entire planet is under quarantine at the moment, it's not true that I'm missing much. But I still would like to keep in the habit of a schedule that is in sync with the natural rhythm of things. "Rhythm" is a really hard word to spell. I tried three times to get that right.

I am making pasta. I am hoping the pesto hasn't gone bad, while also comforted to know that I have another jar if it does. When things are normal and I am working with the kids, I eat pesto pasta every Wednesday afternoon. That's the day that their dad stays home for the day, and I come in early to watch Ama and Chloé while he takes Paul to the British Council for English lessons. He always makes pesto pasta for lunch when he stays home. I really like it, so it's become a bit of a ritual. The first week off of work, I made it for myself on Wednesday anyway—I had a craving. It's funny the things your body gets used to. I am a person who invariably detests routine, but I guess food is an exception.

The pasta is good, except I added too much salt. He never puts enough salt in, so I overcompensated and added too much to my own. It's not every bite though, so all around it's still very yummy.

I eat so much dairy in France. I used to think I was lactose intolerant, because milk and ice cream made me barf. And I used to hate chocolate, too. Now I put heavy cream in nearly everything and crave chocolate like a whiny toddler. It's weird how taste can change. Milk itself still makes me nauseous, though. Milk and mushrooms—I don't think I'll ever like them.

I am going to send you a message. I found an app called Radiooooo and I want to share it with you. I am getting nervous about the words I use. I decided to take a moment to connect with my intention. I wish it were easy to have clear intentions. One intention is that I think you'll enjoy the music, and so I'd like to share it. Another intention though, is that I want to hear from you. So, I think to make my intention pure, I have to be okay with you not responding. It's not that I think you won't respond, I just think that if I reach out with the hope of receiving a response, then my intention will have been corrupted. This mindfulness hash is tricky. I want to connect with my purity. It's easier when it doesn't have to do with you. So I'll breathe for a few minutes. Hold please.

My meditation leaves me with this question: What brings me the most joy? Is it weird that I've never thought about that?

Okay. What brings me joy? I like to help people. That makes me really happy, the feeling that I've done something good for someone else. I like to give advice when it's asked of me. I like to cook for others. I guess I like to cook in general, but I especially like to cook for others. We talked about this before. Natural Provider yadayadaya. I like to write. Less specifically stories, more the general process of writing. I like to feel my fingers create words where before there was blank space. I like to watch these words be typed. I like to watch them grow, letter by letter. That was very intimate to watch. The process of creation borders on erotic. I like to sing and write songs. But mostly by myself. I don't like to show them unless I'm very close to the person. And showing the songs doesn't bring me joy, writing them does. Singing them does. Sometimes I am walking down the street and I start to sing a song stuck in my head, only to realize it's one I have written ages ago. That feeling brings me joy. Learning brings me joy. I love taking notes, I love collecting knowledge. Sharing knowledge too, that makes me happy. I love learning things and then knowing them, and then telling them to friends so they know them too. That is one of my favourite things. I love to paint walls, though I'm not very good at it. But it's still something I love, moving in somewhere and painting the walls badly.

Ah! I forgot the biggest joy of all. I love to fall in love. I love to meet people and be enchanted. I love to bewitch and be bewitched. I love side glances and stomach churns, I love not knowing and hoping, and all that stuff that makes people write poems. I suppose I love looking for love even more than I love finding it. I love to be a lover on the lookout. That's my greatest pleasure, I think.

Oy. Aren't I moving to Portugal? Now I'm talking to you about squatting a chateau in France. What's happening? Am I really so changeable? I mean, there are so many options. It baffles me how I can plan to do so many things at once. I am both planning to move to the countryside with Edie and co, while also orchestrating a solo escape to Porto. How? I guess I never like to keep all my eggs in one basket.

I think I drank too much coffee. I always feel strange after I drink coffee, but usually it is a good strange. Typing feels nicer on coffee. "On coffee." Like it's a drug. I suppose it is. I am a sober girl On Coffee. I guess coffee is better than cocaine.

I'm going to have to sit again. Why do I always feel stressed out after I talk to you? None of this makes sense. Maybe it's the coffee. Hold on, I'm going to sit.

Sometimes I don't know why I do the things I do. Or what I'm looking for when I do them. I am being melodramatic, so I don't want to write about it. But I am hurt, and whether I am being dramatic or not is a non-issue. Also, who is in my mind telling me that I am being dramatic? In what way am I exhibiting drama? I have received a message from my mother. I felt sad when I received it, and now I am a bit sad. And I pull out this document to write my feelings, and I call that dramatic. Why should I be so critical of my emotional responses? In what way does that help me?

Okay. I wrote a piece, a bit of a song, and I sent it to my mother. Her response was underwhelmed, to my interpretation. I became sad because I knew that she would not respond in a way that made me feel nice about what I had written, but I still searched for her to be proud. And that is where the sadness lies—not so much in the feeling that she is not impressed by me, but in the knowledge that I was hoping she would be. I feel guilty for wanting that. And I feel cheated, because she often reaches out to me seeking the same praise, and I give it to her. I don't give it to her because she is seeking it, I give it to her because she deserves it, even if I am aware that she is seeking it as well. And because I don't receive the same affirmation from her, I have two theories, neither of which I am fond of.

Theory 1: Her responses are lackluster because my work is not good.

Theory 2: She cannot be bothered to be interested in the things that I do.

I'm sure there are other theories, too. These are just the ones I am holding within me, now. Of course, she could be busy. But we are in the midst of a quarantine, and this is also very common. I don't remember the last time I sent her a piece of my writing and she responded with praise.

That's a lie. I do. I thought it would be more sad if I admitted I knew the last time, but since I do, I will write it.

It was not last summer, but the summer before. It was when I was leaving Nice, and I wrote those poems about Marmaduke. They were good. I don't know if they're really the best things I've written since, but they are the last pieces she told me were good. She even said it then, "this is the best writing you've done in a long time." So, what had I been doing before? And what am I doing now?

I didn't want to write today. Actually, I didn't write at all yesterday—it's 5 am now. I was reading an article about Freud's theory of seduction. No, that's not about you. It was referenced in a book I'm re-reading called Tender

Points. I don't know what prompted me to go into a 4-hour wormhole of reading about chronic pain and sexual trauma, but here I am. Tender Points is one of my favourite books, it was one of the best things Lou showed me. I don't talk about Lou much, but we dated for two years and hated each other by the end. She introduced me to a lot of good books. Tender Points was the best one.

I don't know why I don't talk about Lou. I think I'm suppressing her, in a way. I don't understand our relationship, nor did I when we were together. We lived together, though—for over a year. I never considered her my girlfriend at the time, but I guess that's what she was. My brain is getting fuzzy when I think about it. I think I've got some internalized homophobia running about. It's hard for me to take relationships with women seriously, but I guess that was my longest relationship. I always say that Augustin was my longest (5 months) and I'm not lying when I say it. I just forgot about Lou, until today.

Earlier I was masturbating, and when I was close to finishing, I remembered the girl from the other night in the window across the street. Then I thought of Ingvild, the last time I saw her. Elsa was on the couch, and Ingvild was laying on the bed across the room. I took a picture of her then, because she looked beautiful. I don't know why I thought of her just then. It happened really quickly—I couldn't even call it a fantasy. It was like those moments when your life flashes before your eyes, I guess. Too quick to comprehend, but you see what matters. I don't know what to make of that. I don't want to think about it too much.

I still haven't replied to her email. I keep meaning to, but I haven't felt well. I guess I haven't felt well the past few days. I've been in a weird place in my head and trying to navigate it, but mostly waiting for it to pass. I cried a lot, considering I don't cry all that often. And I watched the Leftovers, to distract myself from crying. I made a Japanese curry with homemade chicken katsu. That was delicious, I still have some in the fridge. I've been talking a lot on the phone as well, but I'm worried that I'm distracting myself from something. I never know when coping mechanisms turn into avoidance. I'm wary of it, though. Should I deny myself the space to feel heavy for no reason? I exercise. I've been slacking off on the meditation program, but I still meditate in little bursts. Just not with the program. It became something I was dreading, that happened overnight. I don't know why.

I am worried that I'm gay. I think that's a bit of an oversimplification, but I am wondering why that is a worry to me? I have no trouble identifying as bisexual, as I always have...but to be gay seems scary to me. Not because of other people. Because of me, I think. Why does that scare me? When I was in London last time, I saw Calm and Violet together. I remember looking at them and thinking, "wow." It really shocked me, not anything in particular, but just to see two girls behaving as one in that way. I don't know why that shocked me, it's not like I've never spent time with same sex couples. I guess it's because I always found Calm and I so similar, which we are in certain ways. We'd always had a romantic friendship, we called each other 'wife' and we had slept together—but all seriousness of this was negated for me by the fact that we both slept with men, often. We'd go out together and split up to kiss random boys, and see the other later, laughing. So it was light, so it was fun. So we could go home together without the pressure of it meaning anything. But what I saw with Calm and Vi, it was so beautiful. That sounds cliché. But it was. And I was thinking, "Oh. Maybe there doesn't have to be a justification of femininity by proximity of male attention."

I don't think I'm a lesbian, I do like boys quite a lot. But I think I've been giving men a lot more weight in my preference because of the way that I value myself based on that relationship. As in, I see myself spending my life with a man because that's what a life looks like to me. But why? Why do I value myself based on relationships with men who've taken no time to learn about me, to teach me? I can count on one hand the number of men I've met that could match me, at the time. That's not to talk down on men. I am just thinking logically. The things that I value in a partner—emotional connection, creative collaboration, intimacy, etc. etc—I get so much of that from my friendships with women. And because it's easier to blur the line between friendship and romance with women, because 'it's all good fun'—I can have the best of both worlds. That is, fun and intimacy, without real confrontation of self. But that's not fair, is it? It seems that if I like someone, I should dive in regardless of my preconceived notions of what a relationship should be in respect to gender. I think I've been scared about that.

I am going to do something now. It's something I should have done before, but I'm going to do it now.

Today has been beautiful, I'm not at all sad. In fact, I feel quite happy, content. I am reading and lounging, but it has just occurred to me that there is a ghost in my inbox and I'd like to show it out. This sounds dramatic, but it feels dramatic. Or at least, it feels significant. I am trying to remove a block to my recovery. Recovery from you, is that dramatic? More fitting would be recovering from the Symbol that is You. So, I'm tired of reminiscing. I am afraid to lose my breadcrumbs, but I have to stop looking back. So, to look forward, I am going to erase the path that takes me back. Okay, I'm deleting our messages. But first I am revisiting them, to find all the music we've exchanged. I can let go of memories, but I can't let go of music. Or I don't want to. So, let's go back, for the last time. I'll take notes here.

It's a long time to scroll. Finger exercise :)

Yes! We are here. We are then, it is now, I am here. Let's begin.

Kayes Ba by Boubacar Traoré

New Ancient Strings (Album) by
Toumani Diabaté & Ballaké Sissoko

(I've just noticed that this was the most recent
album you've sent me as well. I've been listening to
it nonstop since then, but I didn't realize I'd
heard it before this week.)

Jelike Jan by Fanto Sacko

(You said this is your favourite song in the world)
I tell you:

Check out Paraguaya by Juana Molina

Later, you tell me you've:

been listening to it constantly...

Chimes of a City Clock by Nick Drake

Ces Gens-Là by Jacques Brel

Tokyo After Midnight and Buddha's
Flower by Otto Liebert

Why am I crying? This is silly
I send you:

Ernie by Fat Freddy's Drop

You send me:

Jelike Jan by Fanto Sacko

again. And then:

The Plateaux of Mirror by Brian Eno

I ask:

Do you live in London?

Yeah

I send you:

 Maria Maria, by Santana

I tell you:

It's one of my favorites from when I was a kid

Dope, I'll be there November 9

(What I do not tell you about that is that I am drunk and I have just booked a plane ticket to London because I desperately want to see you again. I have (had) (well still, have) absolutely zero business being in London. I was drunk in front of my job after work, and I took out my debit card and booked a flight to see you. I am like that, sometimes.)

Les Hommes Endormis by Mélanie de Blasio

Do you have somewhere to stay while you're here? You're welcome to stay with us.

That's really nice, thank you. I'd like that.

What I do not tell you is at this point, I am giddy.
I am over the frickin moon. I am (quite dramatically)
ecstatic.

I send you:

Starman by Seu Jorge

Drama by Erykah Badu

Love Seu Jorge

Send me something new. I'm bedridden and bored outta my skull.

I'm in a similar state. I'll try my best. I've been listening to loads of lofi

You send me:

PCH and Erase Racism, by Ol'
Burger Beats

Gradsmoke by Juj

Are you sick?"

No, but are you? Were you in the
hospital?

I send you:

Morning Coffee [lofi / jazz hop / chill
mix] (youtube)

F e e l i n g s (youtube)

Yea, actually I'm still in. I got into a motorcycle
accident with a friend on Monday and messed
up my right side pretty bad... I might have to
postpone my trip for a little while, I'll let you
know.

You say nice things now, but I don't want to write
them down.
Let's skip to the next song.

I send you:

Again, by Slow Hollows

You send me:

An Ending (Ascent) by Brian Eno

I Surrender, Dear, by Nat "King" Cole

What's the Simpsons mix on your
story?

C A L M - Simpson Wave Music
Mix (Youtube)

I reply to your story:

What song is this?

I've been listening to it all day

Orange County, by Mall Grab

Octula, by Flughand

LA Trance, by Four Tet

When I read it like this, there's a story in the
music.

I said I could lose the memories, but not the music.
As if the two weren't inextricable. I am finding more
emotion in recording the transmission of these songs
than in any words exchanged. That is probably my own
neurosis.

December 26, still Christmas LA time

I send you a playlist titled:

Xmas Lux

Still working on order and there was more I wanted to put in, but I have to get ready for a party so enjoy and maybe shuffle it for now.

Sick. I have a thing on tonight, I'll whack this on.

An image of that arcade game just came to mind: whack-a-mole?

I feel like I am constantly whacking moles in my mind, these cute little creatures springing up, but they are so, so bad for the garden.

Wicked, let me know what you think. It's not party music, mostly lofi and noise.

Since you are Gone, these are not—according to the interface, messages exchanged between you and I.

These are conversations between myself and "Instagrammer."

(You reply to my story. Scene: I am in a hospital bed, singing a song I've made up about being in a hospital bed. The song is titled "Me and Bukowski")

If you haven't read it already, I very much recommend Hot Water Music. We all had a really good time with your playlist by the way :) Are you alright? Hope everything's good

I'll check it out. My favourite so far is 'Love is a Dog from Hell'

I'm happy you liked it :) I'm okay, they don't know what's wrong with me yet—I feel fine though. They loaded me up on these trippy pain meds so I'm just writing and listening to music, it's a nice little vacation. Thanks for checking in. Are you feeling well?

I forgot about being in the hospital this time. This was January 7th, 2018. I suddenly wasn't able to walk, I had such bad stomach pain.

I was in the hospital for nearly four days before they discovered that I had 3 ulcers. Stress + booze, excellent combo. The drugs were good, though.

That's good to hear. I'm ok other than, of course, the ever-accompanying downers of being human, haha

The ever-accompanying downers of being human. Memoir or album title?

I think album title is cooler.

Want Me, by Puma Blue

I'm the Man, That Will Find You, by Connor Mockasin

Electric Relaxation, A Tribe Called Quest

Luck of Lucien, A Tribe Called Quest

Bogoróditse Devo, by Chorus Angelicus

Boy in the Moon, by Julia Holter

Minipops 67, by Aphex Twin

We exchanged some words here that are making me tear
up. They weren't negative, it's just the emotion of
memory.

I think it's better I stick to the music, no? That's
what's important.

I am groaning as I read some of these exchanges.
I just shoved my head into the blanket and let out a
noise that I've been making a lot recently. It's
overwhelming. I've been groaning a lot these past few
weeks.

Nocturne Op. 9 No. 2, Chopin

Small Hours, by John Martyn

This is one of my favourite songs. Did you
know the reason you can hear ducks and
the stream is because the walls were really
thin?

Gubélyé, by Mulatu Astatke

I remember sending this song.

I had just moved onto the houseboat in Bermondsey, it
was Easter. My neighbor had invited me over, and her
boyfriend put on this song. I think I flirted with him
a bit (he was really beautiful, to be fair) because
she didn't like me after that night.

I am the Queen of First Impressions.

Soul Lament, by Kenny Burrell

Gary's Theme, by Bill Evans

Impossible Island, by Gaussian Curve

I really have to keep refocusing on the music.
It's easy for me to get flustered like a child,
again.

Do you remember what I said earlier, about nostalgia
and youth?

I am nostalgic for the time when I didn't know how
this would end.

Homebody, by Nai Palm

In between the last song and the next, I had you
blocked for nearly a year. Sometimes I make the
mistake of believing that if I close my eyes, things
will stop existing. I do it less now, though old
coping mechanisms die hard.

#13, Aphex Twin

Xale Bi, by Youssou Ndour

New Ancient Strings (album)

Toumani Diabeté & Ballake Sissoko

That's the end of the music. I'm deleting the
conversation now. Now, if I want to look back, I can
only look here. Now, I have only the important parts.

And then there are days like this, when she comes back.

I'm still with her, but I just wanted to document—
sometimes she is here, and she is beautiful, and I am
happy. I don't have to look for anything from her,
because she is who she used to be, who she's meant to
have been all along. My laughing mother in my ear, I am
so tired, but I will not sleep until she excuses herself, lest
I hang up prematurely and she's different next time that
I call. I am listening to her sing along to "Rescue Me"
while she cleans, she is bright like a child, she is so
animated and it's not just the mania. She is kind and
peaceful and she has fire within her that burns without
danger. Instead, it propels her into life and at last
(again)—she is not just my mother, but my Mom.

I called her because I couldn't sleep. My knee ached so
furiously, I was nearly in tears. I called her, and I knew it
was her—the real her. I could hear her smiling through
the phone, and I groaned to her about my pain, and she
told me how to fix it. I listened, and it worked. We've hung
up now, but my pain is gone, and I know she is good. Not
fine, not managing, she is truly good at this moment, and
it makes my heart swell so much it might break. I didn't
speak much, I let her putter about in her cleaning frenzy,
narrating to me, and I felt my whole body become warm.
I really didn't have anything to say. She sang and I

laughed, and she laughed at my laughing, and I was content. And now I am so grateful that my knee ached and brought me to this moment where I could visit my Mom.

I call her so frequently, as if dropping in and hoping to catch a glimpse of a friend who is always out, but today she was home, and her nasty twin was nowhere in sight.

It reminds me a bit of the priest and his wife, Mary, from The Leftovers. In the story, Mary suffers a terrible accident that leaves her virtually braindead and completely paralyzed. The priest, he takes care of her day after day, this shell of his soulmate, until one day she comes back. For some hours, she becomes conscious again, and they share the love they'd always had. And then she falls asleep again, and he nearly goes crazy trying to bring her back to him. I feel sometimes I'm on this very loop. I check in with my mother constantly, looking for my Mom. And then she arrives, and everything is perfect. But within the perfection, there is the fear and the knowledge that it is temporary, that it won't stay long. And so I don't speak, I don't tell her the things I've wanted to say while she's away. I just let her be, as if her presence is a very fragile ghost that might get spooked if I speak too loudly. And when she goes, I say a prayer that she will be safe on her journey, and I pray too that it will bring her back to me again.

I call her often because I miss her, and because I am tired of being angry, and I am guilty for being angry, but I don't say these things when she is here to listen. When she is here, I am not angry. I forget the feeling altogether—I am a child again, watching my world spin round. And then she says both too soon and at just the right moment, "I'm gonna go now, I've got to try and figure out these cables," and I say "good luck," which is code for: "I'll miss you." So the sun sets, and the night grows, and it is 4:39 am, and it is time to let go.

Forever and always, I am reminded: Love is a process of release.

www.ingramcontent.com/pod-product-compliance
Lightning Source LLC
Chambersburg PA
CBHW071214120626
46546CB00006B/2560